NO '10

W9-BZO-449

Cool
PIES & TARTS

Easy Recipes for Kids to Bake

Pam Price

ABDO
Publishing Company

Visit us at www.abdopublishing.com

Published by ABDO Publishing Company, 8000 West 78th Street, Edina, Minnesota 55439. Copyright © 2010 by Abdo Consulting Group, Inc. International copyrights reserved in all countries. No part of this book may be reproduced in any form without written permission from the publisher. Checkerboard Library™ is a trademark and logo of ABDO Publishing Company.

Printed in the United States of America, North Mankato, Minnesota
092009
012010
♻ PRINTED ON RECYCLED PAPER

Editor: Liz Salzmann
Series Concept: Nancy Tuminelly
Cover and Interior Design: Anders Hanson, Mighty Media, Inc.
Photo Credits: Anders Hanson, Shutterstock

The following manufacturers/names appearing in this book are trademarks: Bialetti®, C&H®, KitchenAid®, Kraft®, McCormick®, Morton®, Proctor Silex®

Library of Congress Cataloging-in-Publication Data

Price, Pamela S.
  Cool pies & tarts : easy recipes for kids to bake / Pam Price.
      p. cm. -- (Cool baking)
  Includes index.
  ISBN 978-1-60453-778-9
  1. Pies--Juvenile literature. I. Title.
  TX773.P534 2010
  641.8'652--dc22
                                    2009025744

Table of Contents

Baking Is Cool

You can bake a pie or tart with just about any filling!

Apple, strawberry, blueberry. Chocolate, mint, pecan. It doesn't matter what your favorite fruit or flavor is. Chances are you can make a pie or a tart with it! They can be as simple or as complicated as you wish.

This book will show you how to make different crusts and fillings. Some pies and tarts are very quick to make. You don't even have to bake some of them!

You may be wondering what the difference is between a pie and a tart. The answer is, not much! Mainly, the difference is in the pans that you use. Pie pans have sloped sides and tart pans have vertical sides. Plus, the bottom of a tart pan can be removed. So, tarts look fancier because you can serve them on pretty platters. Pies are always served in the pans you make them in.

GET THE PICTURE!

When a step number in a recipe has a colored circle around it, look for the picture that goes with it. The circle around the photo will be the same color as the step number.

1 →

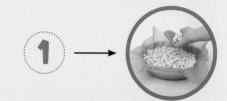

Ready, Set, Bake!

Preparation is a key element of successful baking.
Here are some things to keep in mind.

ASK PERMISSION

> Get permission to use the kitchen, baking tools, and ingredients.

> If you'd like to do something by yourself, say so. As long as you can do it safely, do it!

> Ask for help when you need it. Professional chefs have *sous chefs*, which means "assistant chefs" in French. You can have one too!

BE PREPARED

Read the whole recipe the day before you plan to bake.

> Make sure you have all the ingredients. Do you need to go to the grocery store?

> Will there be enough time? Sometimes dough needs to chill before you form it into a crust.

When it's time to bake, these steps will help you be organized.

> Gather all the tools and equipment you will need.

> Preheat the oven.

> Gather the listed ingredients. Sometimes you need prepared ingredients such as chopped nuts or sifted flour. Do those prep jobs as you gather the ingredients.

> Finally, do the recipe steps in the order they are listed.

Safety First!

When you bake you need to use an oven. Sometimes you also have to use sharp tools. Ask an adult helper to be in the kitchen with you. Here's how to keep it safe.

HOT STUFF

> Set up a cooling rack ahead of time.

> Make sure it's easy to get from the oven to the cooling area. There should be no people or things in the way.

> Always use oven mitts, not towels, when handling hot pots and pans.

> The oven is hot too. Don't bump into the racks or the door.

THAT'S SHARP

> Choose a small knife. Cut just a small amount of food at a time.

> Always keep your other hand away from the blade.

> Work slowly and keep your eyes on the knife.

SUPER SHARP!

In this book, you will see this symbol beside some recipes. It means you need to use a knife for those recipes. Ask an adult to stand by.

Germ Alert!

It's so tempting, but you shouldn't eat batter that contains raw eggs. Raw eggs may contain salmonella **bacteria**, which can cause food poisoning. Eating raw eggs might make you sick. Really sick! Ask an adult if it's okay to lick bowls, beaters, and spoons.

KEEP IT CLEAN

> Tie back long hair.

> Wash your hands before you begin baking. Rub them with soap for 20 seconds before rinsing. Wash them again if you eat, sneeze, cough, take a bathroom break, or touch the trash container.

> Use clean tools and equipment. If you lick a spoon, wash it before using it again.

> Make sure that your cutting board hasn't had raw meat on it.

Tools of the Trade

These are the basic tools used for baking pies and tarts.
Each recipe in this book lists the tools you will need.

9-INCH PIE PAN

9-INCH TART PAN

APPLE SLICER AND CORER

MEASURING CUPS

STAND MIXER

MIXER AND BEATERS

VEGETABLE PEELER

FORK

WHISK

MEASURING SPOONS

MIXING BOWLS

PASTRY BLENDER

SILICONE SPATULA

SPOON

PIE WEIGHTS OR DRIED BEANS

CRUST GUARDS

DOUBLE BOILER

PARCHMENT PAPER

ROLLING PIN

SAUCEPAN

PLASTIC WRAP

WAXED PAPER

TAPE MEASURE OR RULER

GALLON-SIZE ZIPPER BAG

KNIFE AND CUTTING BOARD

OVEN MITTS

COOLING RACK

Convection Ovens

Is there a setting on your oven marked *convection*? Lucky you! Convection ovens have a fan that circulates the hot air in the oven. That makes food bake faster and more evenly. When using a convection oven, set it 25 degrees lower than the recipe says to. Also, reduce the baking time by about one-fourth or one-third.

Cool Ingredients

Butter, flour, sugar. You can make many different goodies based on these three ingredients! Add a few others, and the possibilities are endless.

BUTTER

Choose unsalted butter for baking. You add salt in most recipes. Using unsalted butter keeps the dough from having too much salt.

FLOUR

When you see the word *flour* in a recipe, it means all-purpose wheat flour. But other grains can be ground into flour too. Some of these grains include kamut, rye, buckwheat, and corn.

SUGAR

You use several types of sugar for baking. Most common are granulated sugar, powdered sugar, and brown sugar. Sometimes a recipe may call for corn syrup, molasses, or honey too. If a recipe just says *sugar*, it means granulated sugar.

About Organics

Organic foods are grown without **synthetic** fertilizers and **pesticides**. This is good for the earth. And, recent studies show that organic foods may be more nutritious than **conventionally** grown foods.

Organic foods used to be hard to find. But now you can find organic versions of most foods. Organic foods are more expensive than conventionally grown foods. Families must decide for themselves whether to spend extra for organic foods.

SALT

You may be surprised to see salt in a dessert recipe. Salt is a flavor **enhancer**. It enhances the flavors in your baked goods, whether they are sweet or **savory**.

EXTRACTS

There are many flavoring **extracts** used in baking. Some of these are vanilla, lemon, and maple. You will probably use vanilla extract most often. Vanilla extract is made from the beans, or seedpods, of tropical orchids.

FRUIT

You can use almost any fresh fruit to make a pie. Popular choices include apples, pears, peaches, nectarines, rhubarb, strawberries, blueberries, and cherries. Choose fruit that is ripe and not bruised. If you use frozen fruit, be sure to thaw it first.

THICKENERS

When you make pies with juicy fresh fruit, you need to use a thickener. Otherwise, all that juice makes a soupy mess! Common thickeners for fruit fillings are **tapioca** powder or flakes, cornstarch, and flour.

EGGS

Eggs come in many sizes. Use large eggs for the recipes in this book unless the recipe says otherwise. Some recipes call for **pasteurized** eggs. Pasteurized eggs have been exposed to heat. This destroys **bacteria** in the eggs. Pasteurized eggs are safe to eat uncooked.

CHOCOLATE

Chocolate comes from the bean of the cacao tree. When cocoa beans are processed, the cocoa particles and the cocoa butter are separated. Then they are recombined in different **formulas** such as semisweet, bittersweet, and milk chocolate. In general, the higher the cocoa content, the stronger the taste.

Did You Know?

About 85 percent of cocoa beans are grown in Africa.

Ewww! What's that?

If it is warm or humid, chocolate may bloom. This means it develops a whitish powder on it. Don't worry. It's still okay to eat and to bake with.

NUTS

Nuts, usually walnuts or pecans, add flavor to baked goods. Luckily, you can buy them already sliced or chopped!

Allergy Alert

Millions of people have food allergies or food intolerance. Foods that most often cause allergic reactions include milk, eggs, peanuts, tree nuts, and wheat. Common food intolerances include lactose and gluten. Lactose is the sugar in milk. Gluten is the protein in wheat.

Baked goods can be a real hazard for people with food allergies or intolerances. If a friend cannot eat the goodies you're offering, don't be offended. It could be a life or death matter for your friend.

Cool Techniques

These are the techniques that bakers use. If you can't remember how to do something, just reread these pages.

MEASURING DRY INGREDIENTS

Dip the measuring spoon or measuring cup into whatever you're measuring. Use a butter knife to scrape off the excess.

MIXING DRY INGREDIENTS

Unless the recipe says otherwise, always stir the dry ingredients together first. Measure them into a bowl and stir them with a fork or a whisk.

CREAMING

Creaming means beating something until it is smooth and creamy. When baking, you often need to cream butter. Unless the recipe says otherwise, use butter that is near room temperature.

CUTTING IN

Cutting in means working butter into flour until the mixture is crumbly. Use a pastry blender, a fork, or your fingertips.

MELTING CHOCOLATE

To melt chocolate on the stove, use a double boiler. Put a little water in the bottom part. Put the chocolate in the top part. Turn the burner on low. Simmer the water until the chocolate melts. Stir often.

To melt chocolate in a microwave, use medium power. After 30 seconds, stir the chocolate. Then heat it again for another 30 seconds. You may have to do this several times before all the chocolate melts.

Word Order Counts!

Pay attention to word order in the ingredients list. If it says "1 cup sifted flour," that means you sift some flour and then measure it. If the list says "1 cup flour, sifted," that means you measure first and then sift. Believe it or not, this makes a difference. Sifted flour is fluffier than unsifted flour. This means less of it fits in the measuring cup.

Basic Pie and Tart Shells

Bakers call pie crusts shells. This recipe will teach you how make fantastic pie and tart shells!

INGREDIENTS

2 cups all-purpose flour

¼ cup sugar

½ teaspoon salt

12 tablespoons (1½ sticks) butter, cut into ½-inch cubes and chilled

4 to 6 tablespoons ice water

TOOLS:

mixing bowl
measuring cups
measuring spoons
whisk

silicone spatula
pastry blender
fork
plastic wrap

rolling pin
tape measure or ruler
9-inch pie pan
  or tart pan

knife
parchment paper
  or waxed paper
pie weights or dried beans

TO MAKE THE DOUGH

 1 Whisk together the flour, sugar, and salt in a mixing bowl. Stir in the butter cubes.

 2 Use the pastry blender to cut the butter into the flour. Work quickly while the butter is still cold. Stop when the pieces of butter are pea-sized and smaller.

 3 Add the ice water a little bit at a time. Use a fork to mix it in. Stop adding water when you can form the dough into a ball.

 4 Divide the dough into two equal parts. Shape them into discs and wrap each one in plastic wrap. Put the discs of dough in the refrigerator for 30 minutes.

5 Sprinkle a light layer of flour on the countertop. Unwrap one disc of dough and place it on the flour. Press down evenly with your hands to flatten the disc some more.

6 Roll out the crust. Start with the rolling pin in the middle. Roll out toward the edge. Put the rolling pin in the middle again. Roll in the opposite direction from last time.

7 Gently lift the dough and turn it over. Begin rolling again. Change directions often as you roll out the dough. Otherwise, you will get an oval instead of a circle! Continue rolling in all directions until the dough is 11 inches across.

8 *If your recipe calls for a top crust, you will need the second disc of dough.* First, fill the pie according to the recipe. Then turn back to these pages and repeat steps 5 through 7 to make the top crust. *If your recipe doesn't call for a top crust, you can freeze the extra dough to use later.*

Why Chill Dough

Pie crust is easier to roll out when it is cold. Cold dough also makes a flakier crust. Rolling the dough flattens the pieces of cold butter in the dough. These flat pieces of butter create layers in the crust. The butter makes steam as it melts in the oven. The steam helps puff the layers.

FOR AN UNBAKED PIE SHELL

1 Set the rolling pin at one edge of the dough. Lift the edge of the dough and gently roll the dough onto the pin. When you reach the center, carefully pick up the rolling pin and dough. Position it over the pie pan. Unroll the pie dough onto the pie pan.

2 Gently press the dough into the pan. It should touch the pan all over. If the dough tears, pinch it back together. Using a knife, trim the dough about ½ inch beyond the edge of the pan. Use the scraps to patch any holes in the crust.

3 Lift the edge of the crust and tuck the excess dough under to make a thick edge. **Crimp** the edge with your fingertips or a fork.

FOR AN UNBAKED TART SHELL

1 Place the rolled-out dough over the tart pan. Be careful not to tear it on the edges of the pan.

2 Gently press the dough against the bottom and sides. Work slowly and carefully. Don't cut yourself on the edges of the pan.

3 Trim the excess dough by rolling the rolling pin over the pan.

FOR A BLIND-BAKED PIE OR TART SHELL

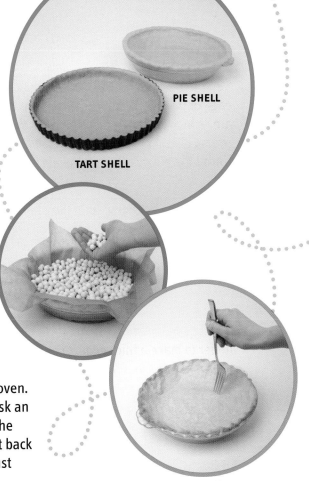

PIE SHELL

TART SHELL

1 Preheat the oven to 375 degrees.

2 Make an unbaked pie or tart shell as shown on pages 16 through 17.

3 Place a piece of parchment paper or waxed paper in the crust. Gently flatten it against the crust. Cover the paper evenly with pie weights or uncooked beans. This will keep the crust from rising and bubbling while it bakes.

4 Bake the crust for about 20 minutes. It should be lightly browned. Remove the pan from the oven. Carefully remove the pie weights and paper. Ask an adult to help you do this! Prick the bottom of the crust with a fork about five times. Put the crust back in the oven for another 5 minutes. Cool the crust completely before filling it.

Baking Tip

Check the edges of the pie crust as it bakes. Cover the edges if they are getting too brown. You can use crust guards (pictured) or strips of aluminum foil.

Pretty as a Pecan Pie

This pie is often served at Thanksgiving. But you can enjoy it any time!

INGREDIENTS

9-inch unbaked pie shell (see pp. 15–18)

1½ cups pecan halves

1 cup light corn syrup

3 eggs

1 cup sugar

½ teaspoon salt

2 tablespoons butter, melted

1 teaspoon vanilla extract

TOOLS: mixing bowl, measuring cups, measuring spoons, silicone spatula, oven mitts, cooling rack

20

1 Preheat the oven to 400 degrees.

2 In a small mixing bowl, whisk together the sugar, cinnamon, nutmeg, salt, and **tapioca**.

3 Peel the apples. Slice them with the apple slicer and corer. Cut each slice in half lengthwise to make thinner slices.

4 Put the apple slices in a clean mixing bowl. Pour the dry ingredients over them. Stir gently to evenly coat the slices with the dry ingredients.

5 Pour the apple slices into the pie shell. The apples should stick up above the crust. The apples will settle and shrink as the pie bakes and cools.

6 Place the top crust over the filled pie shell. Remove any dough overhanging the edge of the pan. **Crimp** the edges of the crust with your fingertips or a fork. Cut several small slits in the top crust with a knife. These vents will allow steam to escape while the pie bakes.

7 Bake the pie for 30 to 40 minutes. Put an old cookie sheet on the rack below the pie pan. This will catch any juice that bubbles out of the pie. Cover the edges of the crust if they get too brown.

8 Cool the pie on a cooling rack. If you can, serve the pie when it is still warm.

The Best Pie Apples

- Cortland (tart)
- Granny Smith (tart)
- Jonathan (tart)
- Pippin (tart)
- Winesap (tart)
- McIntosh (sweet-tart)
- Gala (sweet)
- Empire (sweet)
- Fuji (sweet)
- Pink Lady (sweet)

French Silk Pie, Ooh La La!

This elegant pie is surprisingly easy to make!

1 Put the vanilla wafers in the zipper bag and close it. Roll over the bag with a rolling pin to crush the cookies into crumbs. The crumbs should be fine but not powdery.

2 Put the crumbs in the mixing bowl and add the melted butter. Stir until they are well mixed.

3 Pour the crumb mixture into the pie pan and spread it evenly. Press the crumb mixture firmly into the bottom and up the sides of the pan.

4 The crust is done! Refrigerate the crust while you make the filling.

5 Melt the chocolate in a double boiler or a microwave oven. Let it cool to room temperature.

6 Cream the butter and sugar until it is light and fluffy. If you have a stand mixer, use it. It will make the next step easier. Beat in the cooled, melted chocolate.

7 Add the eggs one at a time. Beat the mixture for 5 minutes after you add each egg. Really, 5 minutes per egg! Scrape down the sides of the bowl every few minutes.

8 Stir in the vanilla.

9 Spoon the mixture into the prepared pie shell. Chill the pie for several hours. Try serving each slice with a **dollop** of whipped cream.

Scrumptious Fruit Tart

Show off your creative skills with this fresh-tasting tart!

INGREDIENTS

- 2 eggs
- ½ cup sugar
- ½ cup lemon juice (from 2 to 3 lemons)
- 4 tablespoons butter, cut into pieces
- 9-inch blind-baked tart shell (see pp. 15–19)
- 2 cups of fresh fruit such as blueberries, strawberries, peaches, kiwifruit, or raspberries

TOOLS: juicer or reamer · double boiler · measuring cups · whisk · knife · cutting board · silicone spatula

1 Put some water in the bottom of the double boiler. Insert the top pan and turn the heat to low. Put the eggs and the sugar in the top pan. Whisk them together.

2 Add the lemon juice and the butter. Continue stirring the mixture until it thickens, about 10 minutes. You just made lemon curd! Remove it from the heat and cool it in the refrigerator.

3 Prepare the fruit. Slice large fruits such as kiwifruit or peaches. Cut strawberries in half. Leave small berries whole. Decide how you want to arrange the fruit. You can use just one type of fruit or a few.

4 Pour the cooled lemon curd into the tart shell. Spread it evenly with a silicone spatula.

5 Arrange the fruit on top of the lemon curd. If you aren't serving the tart right away, put it in the refrigerator.

In a Rush?

You can buy ready-made lemon curd at many grocery stores. You can also use instant custard instead of lemon curd. Just follow the directions on the package. Lemon or vanilla custard works well for fruit tarts.

Glorious Ginger Pear Tart

This tart tastes sweet and spicy. Serve it warm with vanilla bean or ginger ice cream!

INGREDIENTS

3 to 4 ripe pears

3 tablespoons butter

3 tablespoons sugar

1 tablespoon water

¼ cup chopped crystallized ginger

9-inch tart shell, unbaked and chilled (see pp. 15–18)

TOOLS:
vegetable peeler
spoon
knife
cutting board
measuring cups
measuring spoons
saucepan
silicone spatula
mixing bowl
oven mitts
cooling rack

1 Preheat the oven to 375 degrees.

 2 Peel the pears and cut them in half lengthwise. Use the spoon to scoop out the cores. Cut each pear half into lengthwise slices about ½ inch thick.

3 Put the butter, sugar, water, and ginger in a small saucepan. Simmer the mixture over medium heat until the sugar dissolves. Stir the mixture often.

 4 Put the pear slices in a mixing bowl. Pour the sugar mixture over the pears. Stir gently to coat the pears.

 5 Pour the pear mixture into the prepared tart shell. If you like, arrange the pears in a pretty pattern.

6 Bake the tart for about 35 to 40 minutes. Cool it on a cooling rack.

Crisp Crust

Baking a filled tart on a pizza stone helps crisp the crust. Cover the pizza stone with aluminum foil. Set it and the tart on the middle rack. If you don't have a pizza stone, no worries. The tart will bake fine without it too.

Wrap It Up!

Tips for making your own recipes and sharing the results!

> 1 TSP LESS CINNAMON
> ADD CREAM CHEESE (3 OZ)
> BAKE 5 MIN LONGER

Cooks who like to experiment love to make pies and tarts. Once you master the basics, you can try new recipes. You can even invent your own! Try different fruits and spices in the filling. Try different crusts. But be sure to make notes about what you do. Write your changes on a post-it note, and then stick it in your cookbook. It's frustrating to bake a winner and not be able to recreate it later!

ELIZABETH

Pies and tarts are great treats to share with others. You can take them to parties or give them as gifts. Here's an old potluck trick. Write your name on a piece of masking tape. Stick the tape to the bottom of the pie pan once it is cool. That way you have a better chance of getting the pan back!

Glossary

bacteria – tiny, one-celled organisms that can only be seen through a microscope.

conventional – in the usual way.

crimp – to pinch or press something to make it bent or wavy.

dollop – a spoonful of something, usually a topping such as jam or whipped cream.

enhance – to increase or improve.

extract – a product made by concentrating the juices taken from something such as a plant.

formula – a combination of specific amounts of different ingredients or elements.

germ – a tiny, living organism that can make people sick.

pasteurize – to heat something, such as milk or eggs, to a certain temperature for a specific amount of time in order to kill harmful germs.

pesticide – a substance used to kill insects.

savory – tasty and flavorful but not sweet.

stylist – someone whose job is to create, make, or advise about styles. Food stylists often prepare food that will be photographed.

synthetic – produced artificially through chemistry.

tapioca – a food made from the starchy root of the tropical cassava plant.

Web Sites

To learn more about cool baking, visit ABDO Publishing Company on the World Wide Web at **www.abdopublishing.com.** Web sites about cool baking are featured on our Book Links page. These links are routinely monitored and updated to provide the most current information available.

Index